Ignorant Youth

A.M.

PAGE PUBLISHING
Conneaut Lake, PA

First originally published by Page Publishing 2023

ISBN 979-8-88960-432-7 (pbk)
ISBN 979-8-88960-437-2 (digital)

Printed in the United States of America

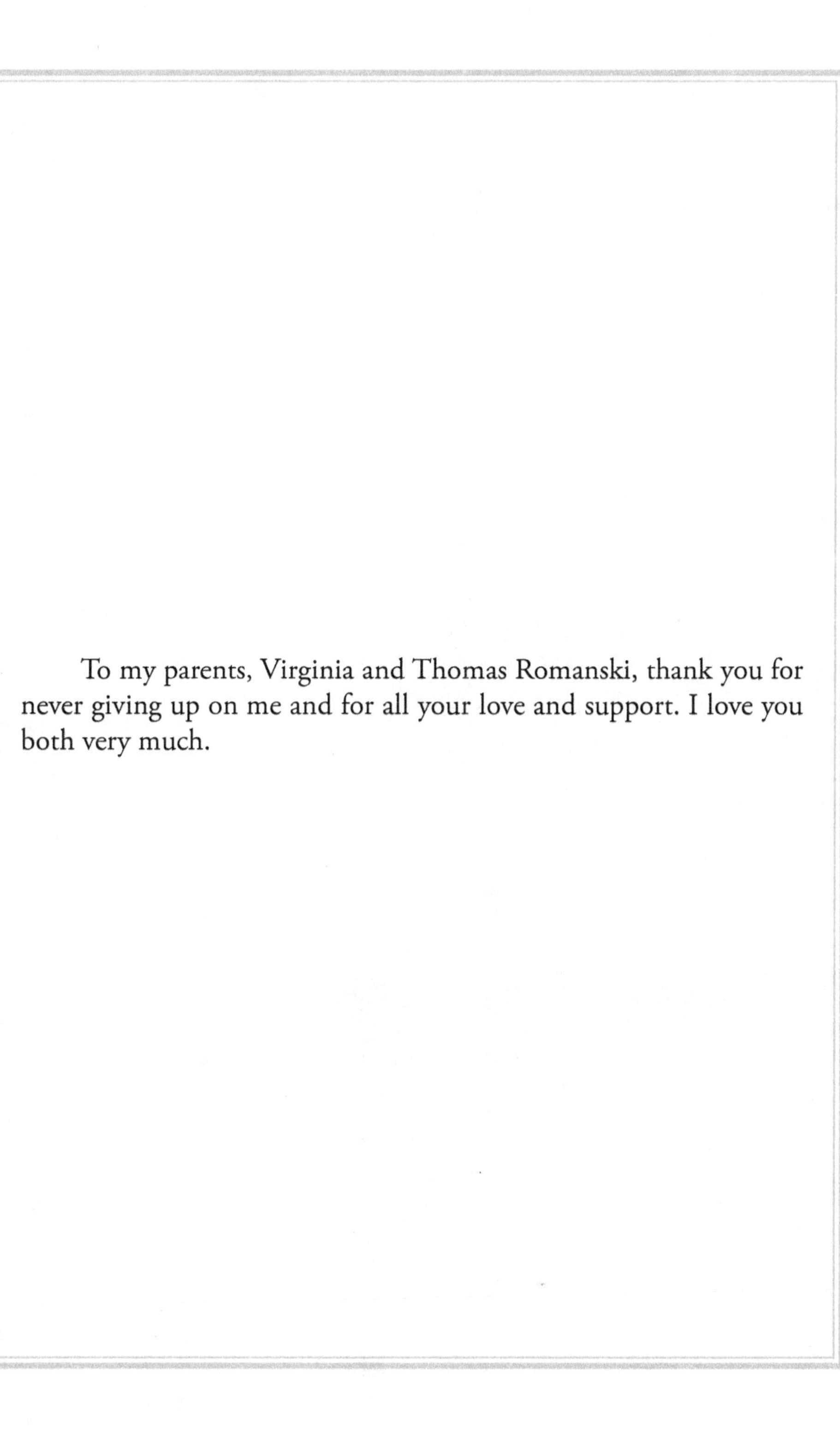

To my parents, Virginia and Thomas Romanski, thank you for never giving up on me and for all your love and support. I love you both very much.

Foreword

The following is a compilation. I started writing when I was seventeen years old. The book is the direct result of bad choices that I made when I was growing up. Our quick rise and even quicker fall have left me feeling useless and alone. To this day, it's hard for me to look in the mirror and see a decent person. I can't have a conversation with someone without questioning their motives. I did something that I knew was wrong, and I knew I was hurting people, but I did it anyway. My friends have met with fates ranging from prison to life-long addictions to even death. This left me with little to no regard for human life, especially my own. The choices you make as a teenager can leave a lasting impression on the rest of your life. Sometimes, learning by experience isn't always the best way.

Acknowledgments

To the Murillo, Chavez, Lopez, and Aparicio families, thank you all for your love and support. To Angie Chavez, Carmen Lopez, Jose Murillo, Richard Murillo, Fernando Paco Murillo, and Tomasa Rodriguez, I miss and love you all. To Christina and Justin, I love you both so very much and I thank God everyday for both of you. To my brother, Matt Murillo, and his family, thank you for all that you have done for me. To my goddaughter, Ashlee Murillo, and my sister Julie Apodaca, thank you both for all your faith in me. To my cousins Mark and Linda Murillo, thank you both for encouraging me to keep writing. To my sister Diana Martinez, thank you for reminding me to walk by faith and not by sight. Ignacio and Lori Chavez, thank you for always making me feel loved no matter the circumstances. To Wayne Riddle, Chuck Dickinson, Jacob Nielsen, Stosh Burchett, and Billy Truex, thank you all for the lifelong friendships. To Tony Aparicio Jr. and Paul Cano, I'm sorry I wasn't a better example for you but I'm so proud of the way you both turned out.

I will not conform myself to the patterns of this world
My thoughts and aspirations I will not put on hold
If a man comes to me and says he'll take me down
He knows not why nor how long I've been around
I've done and seen so many wrong things
I'm not the perfect student or son by any means
I have no fear of man, I will not run
My heart and feelings have died, don't count my tears I have not one

Writing is a great way to get away. For a while, I used it to ignore my surroundings—night school. I guess from the beginning I felt guilty about what I was doing; but I thought I was the only one, so I kept it to myself. I knew what I was doing; and I knew that it was wrong, but I just kept getting in deeper and deeper. As we went along, our reputations grew—mine in particular. Our reputations grew out of defense of ourselves; none of us did anything too bad in the beginning. As we went along, people started to respect us more and more while the respect we had for other people diminished. You've got no idea what it feels like to go from an overlooked nobody to being referred to as "the man." I was actually given spare keys to other people's homes as well as their cars. For me, there was no greater feeling.

Drugs make you think
I wanna touch the sky
When you think too much, you lose all sense
I'm not afraid to die
Anger is built deep inside my bones
Everyone's afraid, afraid to be alone
Money and power are material things
Everyone's greedy, we're all human beings

I was feeling guilty because I was more concerned about who owed me money, and when I was going to get the money rather than thinking of my grandma in the hospital, she died a few days later. I began to see how my friends were with their grandparents—they actually liked them. I felt no real remorse when my grandma died until I was given her wedding ring. When she died, she had forty-two grandchildren and forty-two great-grandchildren, and I didn't think she liked any of us. Then my aunt told me something that surprised me. I guess my grandma had trouble expressing her feelings. That is a trait that is carried on by a lot of people in my family, including myself. Since she's been gone, I've noticed characteristics that some of my family have that remind me of her. I guess she's gone but not forgotten.

Look in the sky, it's the bright shiny sun
Offering praise to the evil one
Organized religions are blatantly feeble
No one can stop me; face it, I'm evil
You get me pissed, you'll pay the cost
Your hope is dead, salvation lost
If you cross me, I'll put you through hell
Forced to pay the consequences, you'll never live to tell

A bad situation turned worse, the first deal gone wrong. He wanted to test the limits I was prepared to go; he found out, and I never heard from him again. I got what he owed me, and he got what he deserved. Looking back, I can honestly say I was a little out of control in the beginning. I think the reason for that was, for the first time in my life, I was the intimidator. I'm one of the youngest boys in the first generation of grandkids, and as nature dictates, I got picked on a lot. Due to that, I probably took my hostility out on people I shouldn't have, and for that, I apologize.

Blessed are those who don't have a clue
Who have no future or know what they can do
The damned and demented shall inherit the earth
We're all liars, sinners from birth
Darkness awaits the damned and rejected
All the world's leaders are truly demented
Gangs kill each other every day in fights
Yet we're still bitching about animal rights

My English teacher was lecturing us about being kind to animals. At the same time, my best friend was recovering from being jumped. He was stabbed in the face. He had fifteen stitches in his head and has a metal plate in his finger where his bones used to be. I thought that the kids at my high school were stuck up and self-centered. To me, it seemed that nothing mattered to them unless they were directly involved. Then it occurred to me: I was no different. I couldn't care less about the school's next fundraiser or football game. What the average high school student knows depends on their parents, friends, and the school curriculum. I heard a few people talk about what happened to my friend, but no one showed any real concern for him. I guess because they didn't really know things like that really happened. These kids had morals and a drive to be something. They were preparing for their futures while we were destroying ours.

Society is overcome by famine and disease
Your world will crumble, fall to its knees
This life you're living has no real meaning
The human race is dying, there's no safe human being
The great unknown lies beyond this life
People kill daily using guns or a knife
Innocent people die, yet it means nothing you see
So live for yourself, and I'll live for me

Watching my friend lie there knowing I wasn't around to help him made me feel guilty. I was only gone for four hours; I still feel like I let him down. From my point of view, I've never really been there for him when he needed me. I bought him his first car and his first gun, but to me, it still wasn't enough. He had all the talents in the world, but he really excelled in basketball. I honestly believe that he could've played in the NBA. I think his downfall was hanging out with me. No matter what I do for him, it will never compare what I cost him—his future. I'm very sorry, Wayne.

You're willing to give your life for the one you hold most dear
What she's holding in her heart is the only thing you fear
She now says you make her uncomfortable, to leave her alone
But the life she's living isn't exactly her own
Her parents and friends make the decisions in her life
Now you search for an easy solution, a razor or a knife
In a normal relationship, communication is a must
The problem is you think like me, there's no one you can trust

A friend bursts into my room looking for anything he can use to cut his wrists. He didn't get along with his girlfriends, parents, and she was in no position to defy them. Watching this relationship made me glad. I never had a relationship of my own. I've been with girls, girls who had boyfriends. I figured if they were cheating with me, what would stop them from cheating on me? You have to have a certain amount of faith to have a successful relationship, not to mention faith in the other person. Seeing and doing the things I did growing up ensured that I wasn't about to trust anyone.

Corruption and deception are all I see
There's nothing in the world to keep you truly happy
The one you love never really loved you
Oblivious to the facts, she was just using you
Now your morbid thoughts are all you have left
Don't run to your parents, they think they know what's best
You now face the cold fact that your first love is all through
The one you held so close to your heart never even liked you

My first observation of love and its manipulative ways. We took turns watching our friend so he wouldn't commit suicide. Losing your first love is always tough, but finding out that he was in love alone proved to be unbearable. Since then, I have been skeptical of women and their motives when they approach me. I don't think much of myself, and in my eyes, I really have nothing to offer anyone.

Everyone's striving, burning to be on top
To college go the richest, the cream of the crop
In school you're classified by how you look and dress
Not by the thoughts you have or feelings you express
My friends and I are unpopular, to say the least
We're treated like lepers or some unwanted beast
I get stared at; my friends get made fun of
These kids talking shit shouldn't think they're above
They've got problems like us but with a different kind of stress
'Cause they'll still strive, strive to be the best

This was written when I was a teacher's aide in a college prep course. The egotism and arrogance of these kids mixed with the fear of failure, and the desire to appease their parents was too obvious to ignore. These kids all had their opinions of me and held me and my friends beneath them. Most of their opinions of me changed when they realized that I was grading their papers. Then all of a sudden, I was "Frank, the guy I hung out with in elementary school." I was sent to a Christian school for junior high, but when I failed to show up to the junior high in my district, they spread the rumor that I was in juvenile hall for a crime spree that my brother and I had done.

The poem is dedicated to Tracy Franklin, who, despite her popularity, was a good friend to me and a very good person. Thank you, Tracy.

The evil moon rears its ugly head
Your hope is lost, salvation dead
There's nothing any of us can do; face it, we're fucked
Kiss your ass goodbye, the world will self-destruct
Religion is a farce, none of it is true
No one will escape life's trials, not even you
God is dead, now merely a marble statue
Only the blind and weak-minded think his words are true

Low self-esteem caused me to lose faith in myself, let alone God. I figured if he did exist, why did he waste his time by making me? Dealing with the average teenage problems and doing something I knew was wrong made me question the value of my life. I was angry at God. I didn't want to take the blame for the mistakes I was making. Watching my friends' lives evolve into what they've become today only adds to my guilt. From my point of view, I ruined my friends' chances for a decent successful future. That's probably why I won't let anyone else get close to me.

We started as friends and still are to this day
Yet things are changing in a very big way
Her eyes are so mysterious and yet so innocent
Every day with her is a day well spent
If this goes any further, our friendship could end; do I take that
    chance
My brain says no, but I fall for her all over again with just one glance

We started off fast, too fast, so we had to get jobs to cover the money we were making. At my cover job, I met a very complex girl who was placed in my life at a very strange time. To the untrained eye, she seemed so sweet and innocent, but her coworkers told a different story. She had faith in me that I had lost. She took the time to find the good in me when I thought she was wasting her time. We worked together for four and a half years, and she became a very influential and important person in my life. My friends began to dislike her—at least dislike the influence she had on me. If it wasn't for her, I'd probably be in prison or dead. She kept me from getting in deeper than I already was. Then like everyone said she would, she burned me. I use this relationship as a template for any potential involvements. I've heard people look for attributes and qualities in people that they themselves have. As for me, I look for the flaws and how bad the relationship will end. I guess I'm a very self-destructive person.

As demons drag your soul to hell
To a world you've never known
Hordes of people are under the spell
Of the one whose heart is stone
Do this, so that or to hell you will go
To a place of pain and torment, more than you've ever known
Are all of your convictions worth it
The church I'm familiar with is undoubtedly full of shit

Observing the way my parents act before and after church compared to the way they act in church was eye-opening. I viewed with skepticism—the church and its followers. Can church really change who you are as a person, or is it a security blanket for those who feel guilty for a week full of sin? I guess a relationship with God is a very personal thing, because from what I've observed in church, these people are no better than me. It's been said, "The Christians aren't perfect, just forgiven," yet their ability to forgive doesn't as easily as it should.

All the church brings is false contentment
But to those with open eyes, it brings resentment
Who invented this deity? Is there really a lord?
Do people go to church 'cause they believe, or are they just really
    bored?
I've been told my whole life that there is a superior being
I just don't understand why he has never been seen
Is he watching the death and destruction of this world?
Is this the rapture getting ready to unfold?

I guess a little blind faith was too much for me at the time. I couldn't believe in someone omnipotent because I didn't even believe in myself. I still have no faith in myself; questioning the importance of my life is common practice for me. After seeing and doing things in my life, I can say with certainty that there is a God. I've gotten out of places and situations I had no business being in, and I walked away unharmed. I know now that God does have plans for my existence, but I still haven't figured out what those plans are.

Venus, goddess of love
Has sent me this desire—a curse from above
Her hair is blonde, her eyes sparkling blue
Could it be this love is true?
Be she knows not me nor of my kind
I don't know what to say to her, nothing comes to mind
To me, she is perfection in the purest form
If I tell her how I feel, I will surely be ignored

A high school crush invited me to a party, so I went. Unfortunately, so did the feelings of inadequacy and low self-esteem. This caused the first of many bouts of emotional abuse that carry on to this day. Questioning your own integrity along with a childhood of being called ugly, fat, and dumb stick with a person. Adolescents are often far too critical of themselves, to begin with, that thinking, coupled with the things I was doing, made me question myself whenever something important came into my life.

Rules and regulations are killing this country
To hell with laws, we need anarchy
It's a free country, yet we can't do what we want
Officials enforce the laws yet still do what they want
Conflicts are rising, this world is too uptight
Any petty disagreement can lead to war, how is this right?
How confident are you in your country's leaders, do you trust them
    at all?
Armageddon is coming, will your country fall?

The arrogance of a new president was embraced by the entire country. It was said to be the second coming of Camelot—he had all the charm and charisma of a past president, but something was off. There were some who questioned his morals and integrity; it turned out they were right to do so. Marriage is a commitment for life, a commitment to the person you love more than anyone. His marriage vows obviously didn't mean too much to him. He cheated on his soulmate and continued to lie about it. This man was the leader of the greatest country in the world, and he lied to the people who put their faith and trust in him. Politics is a necessary evil in this country—an evil I still think we can do without.

As the sun goes down, evil lurks where you least expect it
The greed and immoral behavior of people will make you shit
Earthquakes and famines appear nightly on the news
Heaven or hell, which one will you choose
If money and power are all you desire
Your self-involved world will explode like a ball of fire

Watching and listening to my peers in school proved interesting. Hearing their conversations confirmed my belief that they were very self-involved. World and local events mean nothing to kids, but I guess kids aren't supposed to have too many worries. I spent my childhood trying to prove that I was worth something. I had to prove it, especially to myself. The choices I made back then made me feel like I had accomplished just that. In the end, I realized all I did was trade a childhood of innocence for a lifestyle of addiction and depression—a lifestyle I wouldn't wish on anyone. A lifetime of anger and resentment are all I have to show for what was supposed to be the greatest years of my life, and I have only myself to blame.

Like lambs to slaughter, they do what they're told
None have the backbone to be strong or bold
Each day, they're told, "You must do this to pass"
None have the courage to say "Kiss my ass"
School is like prison, my own private cell
For them, this place is heaven; for me, this is hell

Some teachers tend to abuse the authority given to them. The average student will do what he's told and do it without question. As you can tell, I wasn't one of those students. I got kicked out of seven classes in four years. Although I managed to graduate on time, it wasn't worth the reputation and attention I received. All the extra work of summer school and night school just added unneeded pressure on me. In hindsight, I should've just kept quiet and done the work that was assigned to me. Then again, every decision I made back then was the wrong one. I sincerely and wholeheartedly apologize to any teacher I antagonized that didn't deserve it.

Confusion and death are all I see
Your life means nothing, it changes constantly
Morals and values no longer exist
I'm like your government, I rule with an iron fist
They say love is dead, did it ever exist?
Its purpose was never known; it was all a mist
Love leads to hate, and that leads to me
Don't love thy neighbor and trust nobody

A simple misunderstanding among friends causes resentment and distrust, which still carries on to this day. Business before friendship cost me a friend, but I did what I had to do. I still think I was right. We avoided each other for about three years, then I realized that I was also at fault. I expected too much out of him. I forgot his real purpose. He was my fall guy, my safety net, someone to blame if we got caught. To me, he was my easy way out. It never occurred to me that he saw me as a friend.

Her eyes are dark and mysterious like the midnight sky
Our time together will quickly pass us by
Her simplistic face shines with great beauty
She's often outspoken, at times unruly
Although she dresses common, her looks are never plain
At times, she looks timid; at others, insane
She is as unknown to me as I am to her
Our time together I will always remember

What I remember was her using me to get attention from her parents. They disapproved of me, but at least they were talking to her. Her family was very well-off, so they gave her gifts and money instead of their time. She reached an agreement with her parents before graduation—she dumped me, and in return, she received a new BMW. At least she got a new car out of it. All I got was a lesson in being used.

Although no one's perfect, people think themselves to be
The rich expect you to cater to them on bended knee
They think they're above the regulations and rules
They're just ignorant victims on money and jewels
Whether they know it or not, they're just human beings
These people are enslaved by their material things
They think they can use you and throw you away
But they will get, there comes judgment day

They never really did anything to me; they just believed in themselves. They had the self-confidence that I lacked, and it pissed me off. I actually hung out with some of them; my senior year, they were okay. They tried to fill me with the confidence and a belief that I could actually amount to something. I never took to heart what they were telling me because they had no idea what I did outside school. I felt guilty for trying to better myself when my friends were in their situations because of me. I had to look out for them. They were my responsibility.

The world is crumbling, bursting at the seams
Its sole purpose is to crush all your dreams
Humans feast on their own earthly pleasures
Money and greed are what selfishness measures
How much more pain can this world endure?
The future of mankind is for now is unsure

Get what you can no matter who you have to step on to get it. No one means more than your material needs. That's the lesson I got out of being a teacher's aide in a college prep class. They were bred for this kind of life. They never gave any thought to anything but their own goals. When I asked the teacher why she instilled that kind of thinking in them, she said, "I'm just getting them ready for the real world." I thought to myself, *Who the hell wants to be like that? Coldhearted businessmen are what's wrong with this country.* Later that day, I did something excessive to a man with a family. I humiliated him in front of his wife. All he owed me was fifteen dollars, but I felt I had to make an example of him. I got the fifteen dollars, and I also took his dignity, and for that, I apologize.

Throughout my life, I've not once fit in
My life needs a change, but I have no clue where to begin
I'm not of the in-crowd or of a passing trend
I get ridiculed for not being like others will it ever end
I keep to myself and do my own thing, and for that, I'm uncool
At least that's what I'm told by the blind masses at school
Followers never think for themselves, that's widely known
But I guess in this life, you're with the in-crowd or you're alone

Labeled a psycho because of things I did and was rumored to have done made high school very frustrating. I tried fitting in. In my senior year, I joined the football team but got kicked off the team for throwing a punch at the coach. By the start of my senior year, all my friends dropped out or transferred to a different school, leaving me alone. So I just pretty much kept to myself and ran a very successful business. With no personal attachments to anyone on the school, my business thrived. The people who thought they were better than me began to do and pay what I told them to without question. I looked at it as payback for all the years of ridicule and hardship I endured. Now, I just feel remorse for the kids I influenced.

The most perfect and divine girl stands across the hall
I can't get her attention; she won't recognize me at all
Where she's living, she has no strife
I couldn't possibly offer her a better life
She's all I want and all I need
But she comes from a world of competition and greed
To think she could be interested in me was a foolish thought
I mourn the loss of my love, my love forgotten

The girl I went to the party with was across the hall, cleaning out her locker. I didn't say a word. I started walking over to her, then I thought to myself, *What would she want with me?* So I turned and walked away. We graduated the next day, and I never saw her again. She was a good-hearted person who showed me that not everyone's reputation is earned, and most of the time, it's not even true.

Weak-spirited are those who can't survive
Weak-minded are those who can't think for themselves
Freethinking and independence need to be revived
If you always do as you're told, your life isn't your own
People are like robots; they repeat the same things every day
Then again, learning by experience isn't always the best way
It used to be freedom to; now, its freedom from
Stand up for yourself, have some dignity, you're not that fucken'
    dumb

High school is a routine. It tests your ability to do the same thing every day. It also tests your ability to blindly do what you're told. I graduated but never thought for a second that I was meant to spend forty hours a week for twenty-five years doing something because I was told to do it. To me, that didn't sound like much of a life. Then again, I had faith in a business that was morally wrong. A business that began my downfall.

Life and death are the same fucken' thing
There's no real purpose for any human being
Is the life that you live really your own
You can't change your fate; you're just flesh and bone
You take dignity and pride in your city and school
Yet you have no say on how either is being run, don't be a fool
Be idealistic, reject your school and city
Be true to yourself and endorse anarchy

Graduation night, most of the seniors graduated, and I was actually one of them. Most of the kids I went to school with had no say in their futures. They were given things like cars, money, apartment complexes, and trips to Europe. These things were incentives to keep quiet and follow the path that their parents chose for them. I actually talked to some of them, they weren't too happy with the plans that their parents had for them, yet none of them said a word.

The realm of reality is no longer existent
Due to human ignorance, your life could cease to exist
The bomb didn't exist until feeble minds thought of it
All the world leaders are full of shit
Human could soon be a reality
Arrogant humans never question their own mortality
Our nation's leaders are merely portraits of authority
These self-righteous manipulators will be damned for eternity

How much faith do you have in your leaders? What about other nations? All it would take is a couple of leaders who disagree to start what could potentially be the end of the world. Our lives are in the hands of plain ordinary people—people who can make bad choices and can have bad days. These people use everything from slander to propaganda to get themselves elected. They do everything short of slitting each other's throats to get elected. If they can do that to each other, imagine what they are capable of doing to other countries.

Out of the dirt and soot, the master of evil will arise
Destruction of the world, the lord of the flies
Hell is a land of terror and anguish
Into which the damned and demented are forever vanquished
Chaos and hatred are trademarks of this world
Religious experts agree that this world will fold

It's easier than you think to get away with things you shouldn't even consider doing. There are certain things you just don't do in a civilized society, and if you do them, you never tell anyone. Everyone has skeletons in their closet, things they don't want anyone to know about. Everyone looks normal to the naked eye, but remember, we're all capable of something. The repercussions of my actions as well as things done to me still haunt me. At family gatherings, I hear whispers, people asking questions about me like who I am and what I've done. They usually give me the benefit of the doubt because I'm family. Most of my relationships with my older cousins growing up were shaky at best. I never told any of them what was going on at the time. I told myself it was because I didn't trust them, but I didn't tell them because I knew it was wrong.

There's got to be more to life than that which is morally wrong
I don't know what those things are, I've been out of it for so long
Eternal damnation and physical rejection are all I've ever been shown
Love, faith, and truth to me are all unknown
You feel you've been neglected, treated like a whore
Is this all life has to offer? I want something more

Instead of taking initiative to improve my situation, I did and sold drugs. I used them to make people feel the pain and resentment I felt. I never said it was right. Lack of self-confidence in myself and faith in myself as well as others caused me to take the easy way out. I sat around people's houses doing drugs, and I got paid for it. Making money wasn't supposed to be this easy. Hard work and determination are supposed to get you through life, not deception and revenge. Since those days, my life has been filled with nothing but missed opportunities, rejection, disappointment, and heartache; and I deserve nothing less. I guess it was stupid of me to think that I deserved a second chance at a good life, that I could escape my past. A man's actions always have their consequences, and no matter how long it takes, it will always catch up to them. I'm finding that out now.

I've wanted her for so long
I've waited for her for so long
She could be my all, my reason for being
To the asshole she's with, she's only one thing
If I had one wish, she would be it
She doesn't deserve to be treated like shit
Every day, I watch as she's treated with disrespect and demean
If she was mine, she would be my queen

Feelings grew between me and the girl at my fake job. She kept me from getting in deeper than I already was. She's probably the only reason why I'm not dead or in prison. As she told me more about herself, my feelings for her grew. I always thought that she deserved a better life. I thought I owed her something for being there for me when no one else was; turned out I was wrong. I didn't know her as well as I thought I did. Now, I can't even stand to think about her; turned out working there was the biggest mistake of my life.

These are the four brothers the ones I never had
Don't get me wrong, my real one isn't bad
He just doesn't understand what I'm going through
But the four I mentioned are going through it too
We spend so much time together both day and night
We're always here for each other even with an occasional fight
We're all very different in personality and appearance
Our friendship will never die, not by time or by distance

These four were with me every step of the way growing up. They helped me run my business; they made it successful, but more importantly, they were my friends. I've trusted them unconditionally and wholeheartedly since my childhood, and they've yet to let me down. One of them I lost touch with, one just got out of prison, two others have died in recent years. I know they never felt remorse for the lives they lived, but in my eyes, we all could've done more. I feel responsible for the outcomes of their lives. Even though they never held me responsible for their lives, I would still like to apologize.

In an imbecile's eyes, you're always the same
They don't know what happened but know you're to blame
People on the street stare with shock and dismay
Your family's ashamed of you; you're ignored every day
They assume it's drugs but don't ask what's wrong
You wouldn't tell them anyway; you've been ignored for so long
You're the black sheep of the family; their disappointment is deep
Just like the hypocrites and imbeciles on the street

My brother messed up at his junior high, so my parents assumed I would too. They sent us to a Christian school in Mesa. They took me from my friends and put me in a school to be the only Mexican in an all-White school. Despite what my parents thought I didn't fit in, these were kids. They didn't share the "we're all equal in the eyes of the Lord" mentality that was being imposed on them. With no friends the first semester and nothing in common with these people, I just kept to myself. Going back to my friends, freshman year was hard because I had been away for so long. I couldn't say anything to my parents, no thirteen-year-old has much of an influence on their parents. My brother currently has two wives and six kids. He went from being a problem child to being their pride and joy. They have even asked me why I can't be like him. I thought they had a problem with who I am; turns out they just had more hopes for my life.

Moon is full
Love is dead
People use others just to get ahead
Life is hard, life is cruel
In life, if you don't use people
You're considered a damn fool

Taking advantage of people seems to be common occurrence. Whether it's taking advantage of them because of their good nature of exploiting their naivety. People often jump into a situation with no prior knowledge or experience. To see someone struggle and take advantage of them rather than try to help them gives people a feeling of superiority and empowerment. I thought I was helping people, but all I was doing was getting them addicted. I wholeheartedly apologize to anyone I hurt or took advantage of in any way.

There's no one in the world that we can trust
Our parents turned their backs on us
We support each other's ideas and thoughts
My friends are the only things I've got
If it wasn't for them, I'd be alone
I need companionship, I'm just flesh and bone

Being called ugly, fat, and dumb when I was growing up took its toll. I never thought too highly of myself, to begin with, and my parents were too preoccupied with the birth of their first grandchild to notice a problem, not that they could've helped much. We were doing a lot of wrong things, and we were getting away with all of it. My friends all had girlfriends and girls on the side who were attracted to them. I had personal clients, but I knew they were there for the drugs. I've heard a lot of people say that everyone has a soulmate, a person perfect for them, the other half of them. I guess I just need to wake up and accept the fact that for me, there is no other half. A friend showed me that she helped me realize that a normal, happy family existence isn't going to happen for me. I realized that trying to spend time with people too good for me and trying for things I don't deserve just get me burned in the end. She showed me that too.

Anarchy's the truth; there's no other way
Without drugs, how would you face the day
Drugs make this life of yours worth living
This world is hell; there's no caring or giving
Some look exotic; others, very plain
Do all you want; it just fries your brain
You say it's your life and you live it for you
There's addiction and depression waiting for you

This was written after two weeks of no sleep and after the most devastating event in my life. I didn't realize I didn't have the answer; drugs got me to ignore the pain instead of confronting it. After a few years, I noticed changes in myself and my friends, changes that have had strong repercussions on each of our lives. To this day, there are things and dates that remind me of a day that I don't want to remember. I always tell myself, if I had done the exact opposite of what I did growing up, then maybe I'd be happy.

If I told you I love you, it wouldn't make me weak
It would make me a human, each one is unique
You're the reason I live my life the way I do
My faults and mistakes make me realize how much I really need you
Made for each other, alike in so many ways
Since you've been gone, I live empty meaningless days
You deserve so much more, I realize that now
Without you, I live each day in torment and hell

This was written for someone I never met but whom I love so very much. Knowing my life could've been something so much more than it is always fills me with a sense of emptiness and regret. I know without a doubt that if he had stayed, I would be happier than I could have ever imagined.

My heart is empty; my soul is alone
My affection for her, if only she'd known
Afraid to succeed or afraid of rejection
My life until now has had no sense of direction
She said she cared for me, at least she told me so
I thought to myself it isn't real, the real her you don't know

The girl at my fake job and I kept so much from each other that either of us saying "I love you" would've been unfair to the other. Although she did care about me when I thought no one else did, she also took advantage of a trust I hardly put into anyone. Since then, I've only put my trust in two other women; the first one, I figured, was a mistake. I was right. The second one put an emotion into me that I haven't felt since I was little—fear. She scares me 'cause I'm not used to caring this much about one person. We had a good friendship until I screwed up and asked her out. She felt sorry for me and said yes but backed out at the last minute. She can go to the movies and the fair with other guys, but when it comes to spending time with me, she's always too busy or something always comes up. After the third time she ditched me, I finally got the hint. I guess the person I thought so highly of didn't think of me as a friend but as a convenience or, at times, a burden.

Labeled a subhuman, unable to think or feel
None of their friendship's true, none of these people are real
Told I'm not good enough for her, to stick to my own kind
Like a punk or an addict, a freak of that kind
I pass a mirror, and I look into my eyes
Then reality sets in, and I begin to realize
To them, no matter what I do, I won't be good enough for her
Although the situation wasn't my fault, them it is, I'm sure

My last day at my fake job, I can't even stand to look at her. To me, she was just a shell of a person. She had no consideration for other people, not that she ever did before. She burnt me so bad that it took over three years to even picture her in my head. What she did, though, as common as it is, has been the single most devastating thing that has ever happened to me. Since then, I've been very cautious about who I trust. In the past ten years, I've only trusted and only had feelings for one other woman. All that did was give me a false sense of confidence only to get burned in the end.

Pain and anguish are what you usually feel
Can you be sure that what you're suffering from is real?
Frantically and painfully, you search for an answer
Finding no solution, all you can do is wonder
How will my life turn out, is there a God above
Or is he just a fairy tale like this thing called love?

The end of my business was near. Too many people knew about it. My friends were getting careless thinking they'd never get caught; they began to make it obvious. All I kept thinking was, *What's next?* I just wasted six years of my life. I wasn't prepared for the future. I thought, why did God let this happen to me? I've pretty much given up on a wife and three-kid existence. I was told many years ago that I'm only attractive to crazy women and whores. I realize now that things happen for a reason; God was watching over me. My life could've easily been much worse it is; I'm lucky to be alive. As far as love and happiness go, I have no clue of it ever existing, and I'm tired of looking.

Her exotic enchanting beauty is beyond compare
I've never seen such beauty; I can't help but stare
Instant infatuation, how can I approach her
Why is she with me, I can't help but wonder
Her eyes are dark as if she has something to hide
My brain said, "Follow your heart, it's never wrong," it lied

Trying to start my life over again proved to be much harder than I thought. I surrounded myself with family and did normal things like going to baseball games. That's where I met her. I looked up, and she was smiling at me. I should've known it was too good to be true. We talked and exchanged numbers. Our first phone conversation lasted for over four hours; she knows more about me than anyone. Our relationship was on and off for four years, but like everything else, it blew up on my face. She resentfully told me she was getting married and tried to rub it in. I have nothing against her, and I wish her nothing but the best. When we were together, it didn't feel right. I know she felt it too.

My search for a love like hers goes on and on
My best chances to reach her are now long gone
To hold her in my arms would be a dream come true
But it's nothing more than a dream; to me, that's nothing new
My desire for her continues to grow strong
My heart and admiration to her; they both belong

Although I saw the end of my relationship with the baseball girl coming, I didn't expect it to hurt as much as it did. I couldn't be home by myself, so I called a friend to see if he wanted to do something. He wasn't home but his sister was. She could tell that something was wrong. We knew each other but never spent any time together. We talked at the games but not about anything deep or meaningful. In the past, we were both a little apprehensive toward each other probably because we were both involved with other people. Even though she was going through her own breakup, she took the time to talk me through a difficult time. To know she can care so much about someone she hardly knows made me wish I had met her first. She's without a doubt the most special and incredible person I've ever met. She is without a doubt an incredible woman.

The murky cry of the damned are all you hear
All Hallows' Eve and the end of the world is near
People rarely question their own mortality or existence
Death is coming; you can see it in the distance
Most religions agree that this is the earth's final stage
When you're alone like me, you hope it comes quick, earth's final
    page

Talking with my friend made me realize that there are genuine people left in the world. They're just few and far between, which is why she's so special. She's incredibly beautiful, and her inner beauty is just as amazing. Until meeting her, I never met anyone I could actually visualize spending the rest of my life with. When I sold drugs, I kept my distance from everyone. I used people before they used me; I didn't trust anyone. When they left, I never gave them a second thought. Yet since she left, I can't stop thinking about her. Knowing she took the time to help me and asked for nothing in return blew me away. No one's ever helped me just to help me. It gave me a glimpse of a life I could've had if I didn't screw up my life so bad. To me, she's the very definition of my ideal wife—a wife I don't deserve and a wife I'll never have.

Looking at their lives
Knowing what went wrong
Not doing what they should
Not being where they belong
They say kids will be kids; they'll learn as they grow
Some things aren't worth learning, as if you didn't know
"They're just high school kids" is no longer an excuse
Ignoring their kids and doing what they do is a form of child abuse

Going back to the neighborhood to see that nothing has changed is heartbreaking. Knowing I started it all and left thinking it would just go away by itself left me with a sense of guilt that is still with me. My lifelong friends had wives and kids yet still carried on like they were in high school. They had families that needed them. Unfortunately, they also had addictions and warrants. Leaving the neighborhood was a choice I had to make. I never told my friends I was leaving. I just left. I left them to fend for themselves. I took away their supplier. All they had was an addiction to remember me by, yet when they see me, they're actually glad to see me. I never understood why. I can barely stand to look at myself. I will always feel responsible for the outcome of their lives, and I know I always will.

Standing in front of the mirror
Into my own eyes I stare
I'm screaming, pleading for help, yet no one is there
The struggle now begins, my fight to survive
My brain hardly works, my heart feels nothing, am I alive?
Addiction was no excuse, I never used it as one
I've been around for twenty-seven years; what important things have
     I done?
After visiting with my friends, I realized that could very easily be me,
     I'm no different.

I tried to be a normal person—to get a normal job and have regular friends. At this past job, I was nice—too nice that people actually took advantage of me, and I let them. I was going to be good. I was going to start trusting people. I should've known better. Then I remember what I was told a few years ago: I'm not like everyone else. A wife and three-kid existence isn't going to happen for me. Then again, why should it? Do I deserve it? No. I know I screwed up the lives of people I care about. I moved away looking for a second chance at a normal life, never thinking what they had to go through. I left them in search of a new life while I left them searching for dope.

My family's all here, the tree is so bright
It's Christmas as usual, but something isn't right
A feeling of depression, the fact that I'm alone
Since you and your son came into my life, it hasn't been my own
I never realized that you and your son needed someone to come home to
I always thought rejection was for me while perfection was you
The most beautiful face I've ever seen, the most understanding
    woman I know
The love I have for you and your son, each day continues to grow

In October, I went to my friend's house to give them their birthday presents. When I got there, I learned that the brother moved out, leaving the sister with her mom and dad to raise her son. When we were talking, she hinted that she wanted to go to a movie. At first, I thought she wanted me to leave so she could go see a movie. I never thought she'd want to go with me. I felt lucky just sitting and talking with her, so I left even though I didn't want to. The next day, I called her and asked her out, and she actually said yes. I couldn't believe it. I remember waking up on the day of the date excited. I told myself that I was excited because for the first time in a long time, I wasn't going to the movies alone, but I knew I was happy because I was going to spend time with her. I had to coach my kids that night, so I dropped them off at the park early so I could do something special for her. I bought her a dozen long-stemmed roses. I just wanted to thank her for letting me spend time with her. After the game, I raced home and called her, and that's when she canceled. I felt so stupid standing there with a dozen roses in one hand, the phone in the other, and I was getting canceled on. No matter how many times you experience rejection, you never get used to the pain that it leaves you with. Don't get me wrong, I never expected to be with her or have a relationship with her. I've never been that lucky. I just wanted to spend time with her, but I guess I'm not even lucky enough for that.

The truth sometimes hurts, but not half has much as illusion
Told one thing one day something else the next only brings confusion
Her lifetime of clarity clouded by an hour of self-doubt
An hour alone with her, let alone an evening, is still all I dream about
When face-to-face with her, I can barely remember to breathe, let
    alone know what to say
The time I spent with her and her son torments me every day
I care too much for them both; to me, that much is clear
Living another year without them both is the only thing I fear

After somewhat recovering from being ditched by this girl, we were talking on the phone, and her son was crying in the background. He was teething. When we hung up, I bought him pain reliever and a teether. I couldn't just sit home knowing he was in pain. When I got to her house, she was sitting in a gliding chair with the baby in her lap. I looked up, and the most beautiful face in the world was looking at me, smiling. My first thought was that I'd love to come home to that every day for the rest of my life, then I thought she didn't even want to go to a movie with me let alone spend her life with me.

I bought an extra ticket for every baseball game I went to that year for her, but I never called her. I didn't think she'd want to go with me. Don't get me wrong, I'm used to rejection. I don't look forward to it, but I always expect it. I always wanted to coach her son in baseball, to be there for him, and to watch him grow up. Now, I'd settle for seeing them for ten minutes. I'd give up the rest of my life to spend just one day with her and her son. I know she doesn't know how I feel, but given her hints, it probably wouldn't matter to her anyway.

If ignorance is bliss, then why am I in hell
It started so different this time, the end I know all too well
Her false interest, false concern was mistaken for genuine affection
The more faith I put in her, the more I experience rejection
I never got to hold her in my arms or touch her beautiful face
She knows she's too good for me; my past is a disgrace
She unexpectedly reentered my life only to leave again just as fast
The love of my life is walking away again; my time with her has
    passed

I dropped my cousins off at the state fair, and they saw her there. She asked if I was there and how I was doing. She asked my cousin, "He doesn't do this kind of stuff, huh?" I told her before that I don't drink or go to bars. I guess because of that, she assumed I was some kind of shut in or something. In the short time she was back in my life, she said I could see her two separate times. She said she'd let me know when we could meet; she never did. I guess "Kill them with kindness" isn't just a saying for her. When I sold drugs, I was told, "Never give anyone a second chance. No one deserves a second chance. All that does is give them a chance to fuck you over again, and no one fucks me over twice!" To me, that makes sense; but when it comes to her, I lose all sense. I've been told that good things happen to good people. I guess for people like me, we also get what we deserve. I guess she was put in my life to prove to me that I do have a heart and that she's capable of breaking it over and over again.

And so the saying goes: "Nothing ventured, nothing gained"
I figured I had nothing to lose; I thought nothing I valued remained
I was told long ago, once a fool always a fool
Fate and God played a joke on me; it was nothing less than cruel
False hope a drop of confidence and a lonely beautiful woman
I took the bait without any thought of what always happens in the
    end
With her confidence renewed, she expectantly backed out
It was both the best and worst day for me in nine years without a
    doubt
I should've seen it coming; she's the most beautiful woman you'll
    ever see
She could have anyone in the world she wants; what would she want
    with me?

It's been over a year since I've seen her, and I'm getting used to it. I don't like it, but I'm getting used to it. I still wake up every day hoping to see her and her son, but I guess for the ignorant, hope springs eternal. I guess Blaise Pascal said it best when he said, "The heart has reasons which reason can't understand." This last rejection sent me running back to the only thing I ever did successfully, the only thing I was ever good at.

Conclusion

When I was little, I used to play football in the front yard with my big brother and two older cousins. We all dreamed of playing football for the Los Angeles Rams when we grew up. We never thought our lives would end up like this. My cousin with various addictions, an unspecified number of kids, and a very short temper. My brother with two wives, six kids, hidden insecurities, and trust issues that are very well justified. My other cousin is a convicted felon who used to take what he wanted rather than work for it. He also couldn't keep his hands to himself, and because of that, he's been exiled from our family for over four years. Then there's the youngest—me. I have no career, no family, no prospects, and no hope. Something I looked at as a summer job has left me with a lifetime of problems. Problems very few people can understand and affiliations I never imagined. I've done and seen things that people couldn't even begin to comprehend. These things are still with me; they still haunt me. Growing up, the last thing any child needs to hear is a negative comment. Things like "What's wrong with you?" "Why aren't you normal?" and "Every time we talk, I get more and more depressed" are things I've heard all my life. Those comments drove me further and further away. Now, it's too late. I'm in too deep. I have no one to help me, and I don't think anyone could. As little as a year and a half ago, I dreamed of a normal life. A life with a beautiful woman and her handsome son. The woman is the most beautiful woman in the world to me. She can light up any room with her gorgeous smile. I could look into her amazing eyes, and all my problems just don't matter anymore. Now, she's gone. All I have left are pictures. Pictures of my last chance at a normal life—the chance I never got. I know there's no point to it, and all it does is bring back the heartache, but there are times when I still dream about her. I dream of holding her, looking into her eyes, laying down beside her, and touching her beautiful face. I dream of falling asleep on the couch with her son in my arms. I dream of taking him to Dodger Stadium and to football games to watch the Rams play. I even dream of staying up late and taking care of him when he's sick. I know that marriage and kids can be trying, but compared to what I've been through, it would be a dream come true. Yet nothing's changed; it's still just a dream. My reality is very different. I sleep with one eye open every night. Everywhere I go, I'm constantly looking over my shoulder, wondering how, when, and sometimes even praying it will all go wrong. Every day, I wake up wishing I was someone else, someone good. Each day, I watch as people take things for granted, things I'll never experience. Things like waking up next to the person that means more to you than anyone else, playing with their children, watching them as they learn and grow. To know you're important, that you're needed, that you belong—these things are foreign to me as they probably should be. Money, power, respect—none of these things were worth my life, a life now out of reach. In closing to my younger cousins, my nephew, and nieces, you all have the talent and ability to be anything you want. Please don't jeopardize that.

About the Author

A. M. was born in Phoenix, Arizona, where he lives to this day. He enjoys the peace and quiet of living alone, spending time with God by praying and reading the Bible, and spending time with family.